The ICKY BUG
Alphabet Book

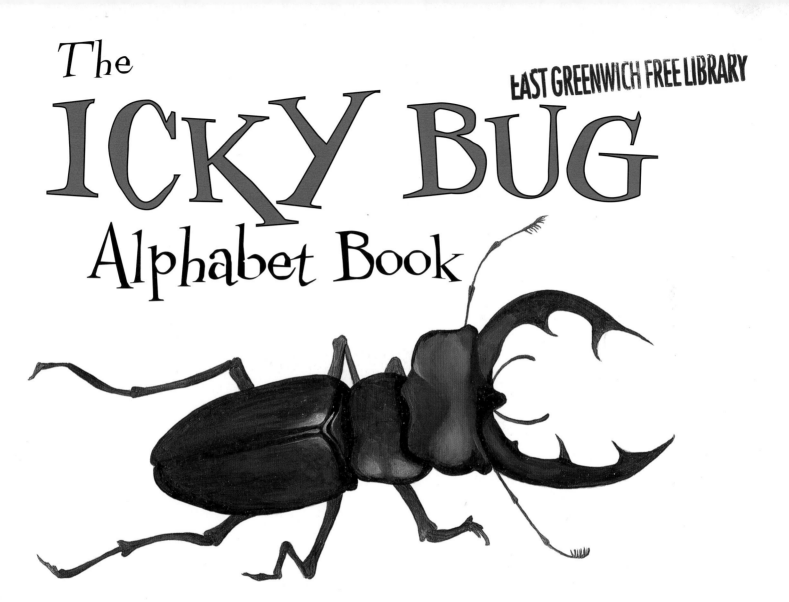

Jerry Pallotta ● Illustrated by Ralph Masiello

ini Charlesbridge

For Julia, Joey III, Jimmy, Lauren, Jenna, A.J., Lisa, Bobby, Johnny, Alison, David, Jr., Lady
Diane, Christine, Elizabeth, Emily, Andrew, Meaghan, Daniel, Jr., T.T., Lyndsay, Steven, Kaleigh,
Sheila, Neil, Eric, Jill, Brittany, Meghan, Nicholas, Timmy, Abby, Hannah, Emma, and . . .
—J. P.

Published by Charlesbridge
85 Main Street, Watertown, MA 02472
(617) 926-0329 • www.charlesbridge.com

Library of Congress Cataloging-in-Publication Data
Pallotta, Jerry.
   The icky bug alphabet book / by Jerry Pallotta; Ralph Masiello,
illustrator.
      p.   cm.
   Summary: Introduces the characteristics and activities of insects and
other crawly creatures from A to Z, beginning with the ant and concluding
with the zebra butterfly.
   ISBN-13: 978-0-88106-456-8 (reinforced for library use)
   ISBN-10: 0-88106-456-4 (reinforced for library use)
   ISBN-13: 978-0-88106-450-6 (softcover)
   ISBN-10: 0-88106-450-5 (softcover)
1. Insects—Juvenile literature. 2. English language—Alphabet—Juvenile
literature. [1. Insects. 2. Alphabet.] I. Masiello, Ralph, ill. II. Title.
QL467.2.P32   1986b
595.7—dc20   89-60421

Printed in Korea
(hc) 10 9 8 7 6 5 4 3 2
(sc) 10 9 8 7 6 5 4

Although the general public considers every creature in
this book a bug, in fact only the Yellow Plant Bug and
the Cotton Stainer are true bugs. The Velvet Mite and
the Scorpion are arachnids. The Orb Weaver, Water
Spider, and Tarantula are spiders, a specific type of
arachnid. The rest, including the true bugs, are insects.

A a

A is for Alphabet Book.
A is also for Ant. Ants are hard
workers. Ants are able to carry
things that are larger and heavier
than they are. They always seem
to be trying to build something.

B b

B is for Bumblebee. Because the Bumblebee is furry, it is able to stay outside in cooler weather than other types of bees. Bumblebees fly from flower to flower collecting nectar to make honey.

C c

C is for Cricket. The Cricket likes to hide under things. It makes noise by rubbing its wings together. Isn't it fun to listen to lots of Crickets at night?

D d

D is for Dragonfly. The Dragonfly has four wings. When Dragonflies stop flying and take a rest, they are unable to fold their wings back.

E is for Earwig. No one seems to know how the Earwig got its name. It does not crawl into people's ears. It has a pincher at the tail end of its body.

E e

F f

F is for Firefly. Fireflies shine like lightbulbs in the dark. When they light up, they can find each other more easily. Fireflies are easy to catch because they fly so slowly.

G is for Grasshopper. Grasshoppers can jump really well. If you try to catch one, it will usually jump away just as you are about to touch it.

Gg

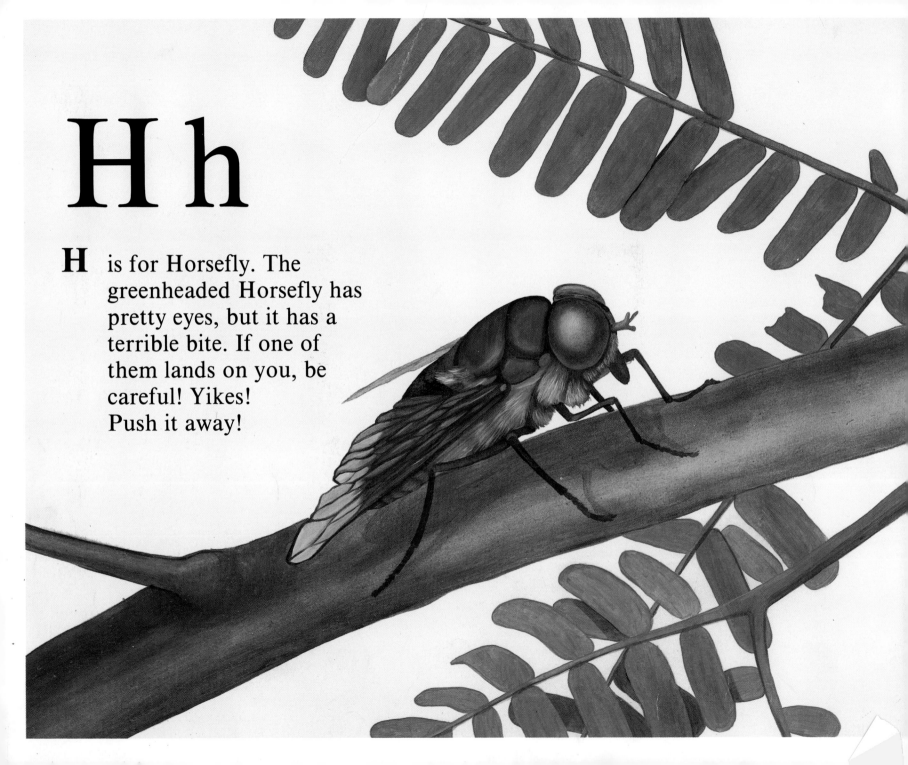

H h

H is for Horsefly. The greenheaded Horsefly has pretty eyes, but it has a terrible bite. If one of them lands on you, be careful! Yikes! Push it away!

I is for Io Moth. The Io Moth has two spots on its lower wings that look like eyes. When birds go near these moths and see the spots, they become startled and fly away.

Ii

J j

J is for Japanese Beetle. These beetles love to eat flowers. Sometimes they eat so much that they cause lots of damage to plants.

K k

K is for Katydid. Katydids, like crickets, make noise by rubbing their wings together. The noise they make sounds like their name. "Ka-ty-did, Ka-ty-did, Ka-ty-did!" Sometimes they say "Ka-ty-didn't."

L l

L is for Ladybug. This insect is really called a Ladybird Beetle. They are so round, it is hard to believe that they can fly. But they can.

M is for Monarch. The Monarch Butterfly is known for migrating. It flies from the northern United States all the way to Mexico. Birds know that Monarchs taste awful, so they never go near them.

M m

N n

N is for No-see-ums. No-see-ums is a word for tiny insects that are almost impossible to see. They are flies that are really called midges. They can make people miserable because they bite.

O is for Orb Weaver. Spiders that make round orb shaped webs are called Orb Weavers. Many people are frightened by spiders, but most of them will not hurt you.

P is for Praying Mantis. It is called a Praying Mantis because it looks like it is kneeling and praying. Gardeners and farmers like them because they eat pesty bugs that are harmful to vegetables and other plants.

P p

Q is for Queen Bee. In a bee hive there is only one Queen Bee. She can lay thousands of eggs per day. All of the other bees in the hive take good care of the Queen Bee.

Qq

R r

R is for Red Admiral. This butterfly is not bright red like an apple or a cherry. It is a rusty orange color. Red Admirals are very difficult to catch because they fly fast and erratically.

S s

S is for Scorpion. Scorpions are really scary looking. They have two front pinchers just like lobsters. At the end of their tails, they have stingers. Would you like to be stung by a Scorpion?

T t

T is for Tarantula. The Tarantula is a big furry spider. It can grow to be as large as your hand. Tarantulas and Scorpions are found in warm climates.

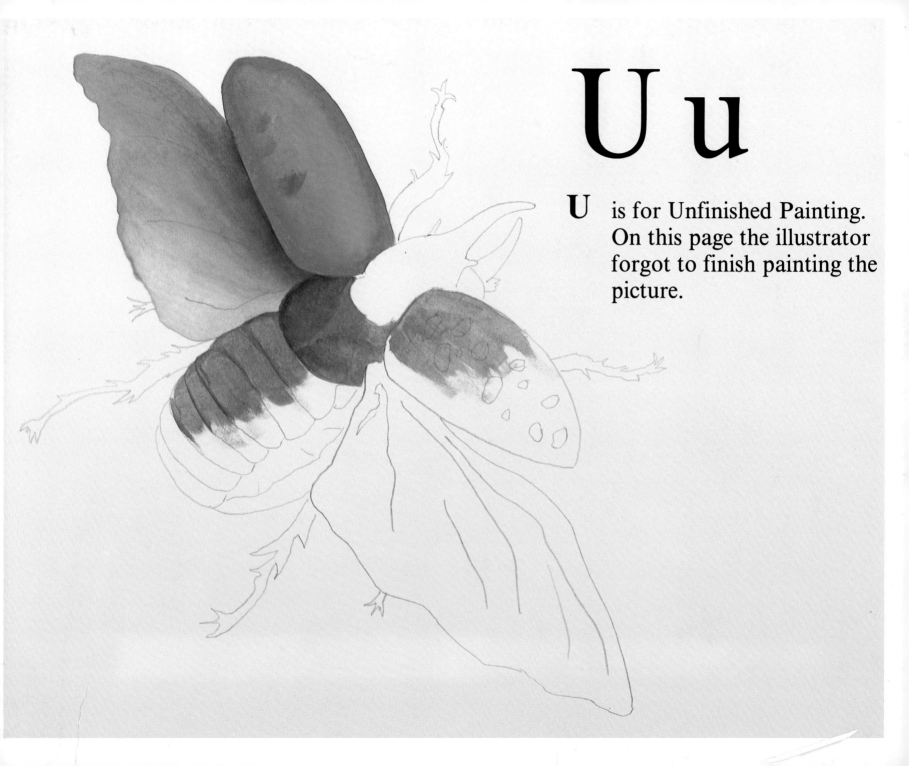

U u

U is for Unfinished Painting. On this page the illustrator forgot to finish painting the picture.

U u

U is for Unicorn Beetle. O.K., that's better. Now the illustrator has finished the painting. The Unicorn Beetle has a single horn sticking out of its head.

V v

v is for Velvet Mite. These creatures are red and so small that you can hardly see them. About thirty of them could fit on the fingernail of your thumb.

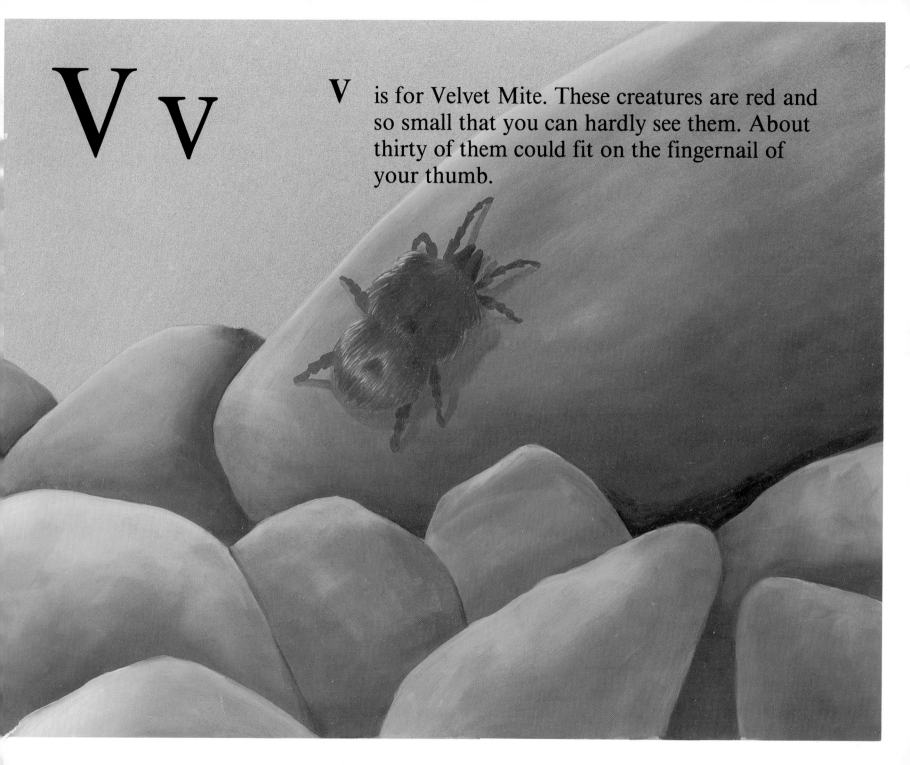

W is for Water Spider. This spider makes its home underwater. It weaves a special web which allows it to bring air under the water. It catches and eats things that swim or float nearby.

W w

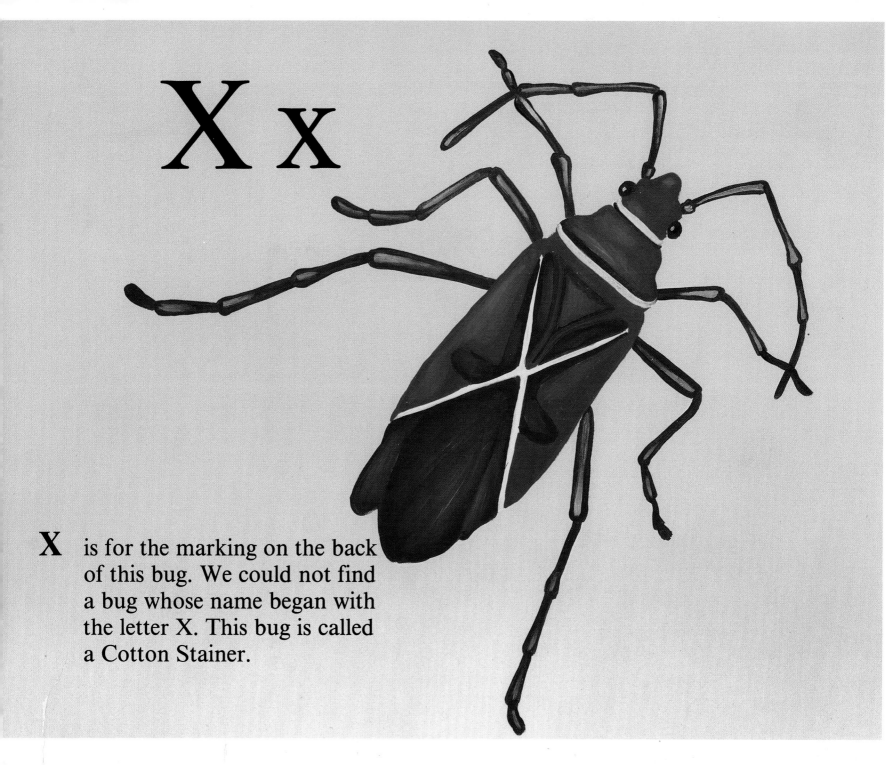

X x

X is for the marking on the back of this bug. We could not find a bug whose name began with the letter X. This bug is called a Cotton Stainer.

Y is for Yellow Plant Bug. This bug is very easy to see because it is a bright color. It has six legs just like all other insects.

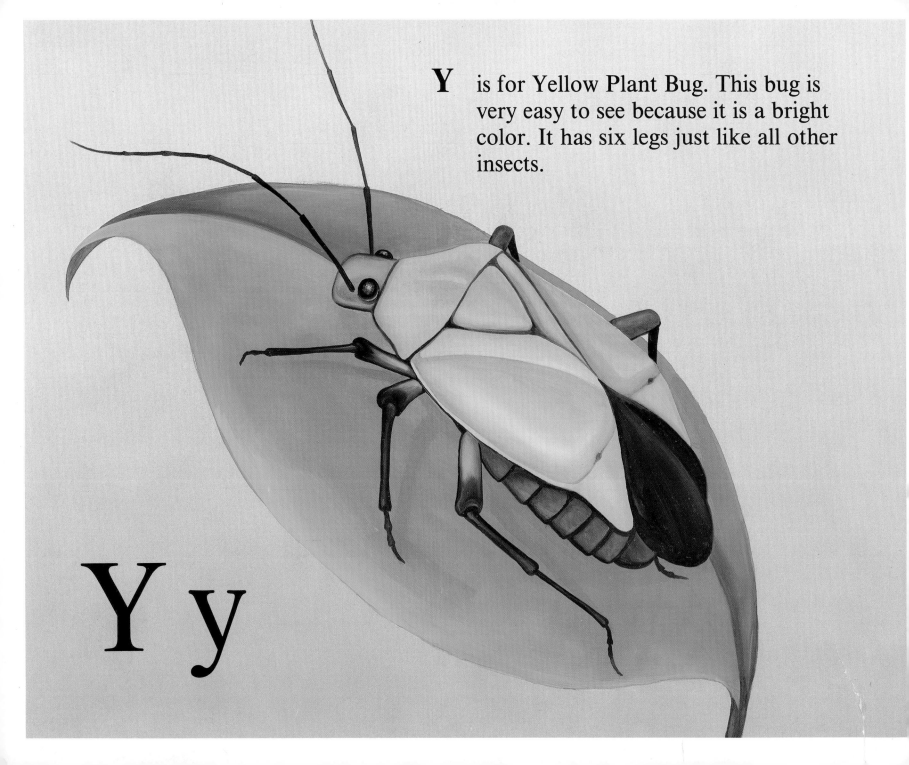

Y y

Z z

Z is for Zillions of Zebra Butterflies. Zillions of them flying all at once would be a beautiful sight to see.

Now that we have gone through
the alphabet, on this page are some
WICKED ICKY BUGS.

Although the general public considers every creature in this book a bug, in fact, only the Yellow Plant Bug and the Cotton Stainer are true bugs. The Orb Weaver, Water Spider and Tarantula, are spiders. The Velvet Mite and the Scorpion are arachnids. The rest, including the true bugs, are insects.